T0010020

# MBA VS.
## ARACAL

NATHAN SOMMER

*TORQUE*™

EDIA • MINNEAPOLIS, MN

™

Torque brims with excitement
perfect for thrill-seekers of all kinds.
Discover daring survival skills, explore
uncharted worlds, and marvel at mighty
engines and extreme sports. In *Torque* books,
anything can happen. Are you ready?

This edition first published in 2024 by Bellwether Media, Inc.

No part of this publication may be reproduced in whole or in part without written
permission of the publisher. For information regarding permission, write to
Bellwether Media, Inc., Attention: Permissions Department,
6012 Blue Circle Drive, Minnetonka, MN 55343.

Library of Congress Cataloging-in-Publication Data

LC record for Black Mamba vs. Caracal available at:
https://lccn.loc.gov/2023042540

Text copyright © 2024 by Bellwether Media, Inc. TORQUE and associated logos are
trademarks and/or registered trademarks of Bellwether Media, Inc.

Editor: Suzane Nguyen        Designer: Josh Brink

Printed in the United States of America, North Mankato, MN.

# TABLE OF CONTENTS

# THE COMPETITORS

Africa's deserts and grasslands are home to many **predators.** Black mambas can defeat most of them with their **venomous** bite! They are one of the world's deadliest snakes.

Caracals are another top predator. These cats are silent hunters. They sneak up and pounce on their **prey**. Which of these predators rules the **savanna**?

# BLACK MAMBA PROFILE

**LENGTH**
UP TO 14 FEET
(4.3 METERS)

**WEIGHT**
UP TO 3.5 POUNDS
(1.6 KILOGRAMS)

| 0 | 3 FEET | 6 FEET | 9 FEET | 12 FEET | 15 FEET |

**HABITAT**

FORESTS

GRASSLANDS

SAVANNAS

DESERTS

**BLACK MAMBA RANGE**

■ RANGE

Black mambas are one of Africa's longest snakes. They grow up to 14 feet (4.3 meters) long. The snakes have thin, grayish-brown bodies with white underbellies.

Black mambas are found throughout southern and eastern Africa. The snakes prefer savannas and grasslands. They often make homes in termite mounds and under fallen trees.

## ALL IN A NAME

Black mambas are named after the black color inside their mouths.

Caracals are small wild cats. They have long legs and reddish-brown fur. Their large, pointed ears are topped with long, black **tufts**. The tufts may help them hear and **communicate**.

Caracals are found throughout the Middle East, Africa, and parts of Asia. These **solitary** cats make **territories** in savannas, deserts, and forests. They are **nocturnal** hunters. They look for meals at night.

# CARACAL PROFILE

**LENGTH**
UP TO 3.5 FEET
(1.1 METERS)

**WEIGHT**
UP TO 44 POUNDS
(20 KILOGRAMS)

0     2 FEET     4 FEET     6 FEET

**HABITAT**

SAVANNAS     DESERTS     FORESTS

**CARACAL RANGE**

☐ RANGE

# SECRET WEAPONS

Black mambas are one of the world's fastest snakes. They slither at speeds of up to 12.5 miles (20.1 kilometers) per hour. This helps them escape enemies.

## HUNTING PARTNERS

Humans train caracals to catch food for them in some parts of the world.

Caracals are built for sneak attacks. Their reddish-brown fur works as **camouflage** to help them stay hidden. Fur under their feet makes their footsteps silent as they approach prey.

# BLACK MAMBA VENOM

| | |
|---|---|
| BLACK MAMBA VENOM:<br>UP TO 20 DROPS PER FANG | 💧💧💧💧💧💧💧💧💧💧<br>💧💧💧💧💧💧💧💧💧💧 |
| DEADLY TO HUMANS:<br>2 DROPS | 💧💧 |

FANGS

Black mambas have sharp **fangs** at the front of their mouths. They use these fangs to strike and bite prey quickly. Each fang carries up to 20 drops of venom.

# CARACAL LEAPING HEIGHT

12 FEET

9 FEET

6 FEET

3 FEET

0 FEET

BASKETBALL HOOP
10 FEET (3 METERS)

CARACAL
10 FEET (3 METERS)

Caracals' long back legs give them amazing jumping power. The cats can leap up to 10 feet (3 meters) high. They can catch birds in midair!

# SECRET WEAPONS

SPEED     SHARP FANGS     VENOM

Black mambas have deadly venom in their bites. Venom from one bite can defeat large animals. First it stops prey from moving. Then it stops the prey's heart!

**CARACAL**

CAMOUFLAGE       LONG LEGS       CLAWS

Caracals use thick, razor-like claws to defeat prey. Their claws also help them easily climb trees. The cats keep their claws sharp by scratching them on trees.

# ATTACK MOVES

Black mambas attack when cornered.
They raise their bodies off the ground. Then they
open their mouths and hiss to warn enemies.
If enemies do not leave, the black mamba strikes!

## STASHED PREY

Caracals often store unfinished meals in hollow trees or bushes. This allows them to feed on prey several times.

Caracals hunt whatever they can catch. They **stalk** their prey using silent footsteps. The cats wait for the perfect moment to **ambush**. Then, they pounce!

Black mambas sink their fangs into prey to release venom. They often bite enemies multiple times. The snakes swallow small prey whole!

## ACT FAST

Without treatment, bites from black mambas become deadly for humans within 20 minutes.

Caracals first wound prey with swipes from their claws. Then they defeat it with bites to the neck. Caracals attack the throats of large prey. They bite smaller prey behind the neck.

# READY, FIGHT!

A caracal accidentally steps on a sleeping black mamba. The snake wakes up. It raises its head and hisses. The caracal pounces on and scratches the black mamba.

The snake quickly bites the caracal. Soon the venom stops the caracal from moving. The caracal was no match for the mamba's deadly bite!

# GLOSSARY

**ambush**—to carry out a surprise attack

**camouflage**—colors and patterns that help an animal hide in its surroundings

**communicate**—to share thoughts and feelings using sounds, faces, and actions

**fangs**—long, sharp teeth

**nocturnal**—active at night

**predators**—animals that hunt other animals for food

**prey**—animals that are hunted by other animals for food

**savanna**—a flat grassland in Africa with very few trees

**solitary**—related to living alone

**stalk**—to follow closely and quietly

**territories**—home areas that animals defend

**tufts**—thick patches of fur

**venomous**—able to produce venom; venom is a kind of poison made by some snakes.

# TO LEARN MORE

## AT THE LIBRARY

Culliford, Amy. *Black Mamba*. New York, N.Y.: Crabtree Publishing, 2022.

Downs, Kieran. *King Cobra vs. Mongoose*. Minneapolis, Minn.: Bellwether Media, 2022.

Winter, Steve, and Sharon Guynup. *The Ultimate Book of Big Cats*. Washington, D.C.: National Geographic Kids, 2022.

## ON THE WEB

**FACTSURFER**

Factsurfer.com gives you a safe, fun way to find more information.

1. Go to www.factsurfer.com

2. Enter "black mamba vs. caracal" into the search box and click 🔍.

3. Select your book cover to see a list of related content.

# INDEX

The images in this book are reproduced through the courtesy of: suebg1 photography/ Getty Images, front cover (black mamba head); Svetography, cover (caracal); Craig Cordier/ Getty Images, pp. 2-3, 6-7, 10, 14 (speed), 16, 20-21, 22-24; Shumba138, pp. 2-3, 14, 20-21, 22-24; WS.photo, pp. 2-3, 20-21, 22-24; imageBROKER/M. Dobiey/ Alamy, p. 4; Régis Cavignaux/ Superstock, p. 5; Stu Porter, pp. 8-9, 15 (main, long legs, claws); CHROMORANGE / Günter Fischer/ Alamy, p. 11; Michael D. Kern/ Nature Picture Library, p. 12; Austin J. Stevens/ agefotostock, pp. 12 (fangs), 14 (fangs); Rich Lindie, p. 13; reptiles4all, p. 14 (venom); Tomas Drahos, p. 15 (camouflage); imageBROKER/ Newscom, p. 17; Karl H. Switak/ Science Source Images, p. 18; Martin Harvey/ Getty Images, p.19.